C.S. Lewis

A Critical Essay
by Peter Kreeft

Christendom College Press
Front Royal, Virginia

For
WILLIAM HARRY JELLEMA:
A Wise Man

The following publishers have kindly granted permission to quote from their publications here named: Cambridge University Press, *The Discarded Image* by C.S. Lewis; Dodd, Mead & Company, *Orthodoxy* by G.K. Chesterton; Houghton Mifflin Company, *Tree and Leaf* by J.R.R. Tolkien; Harcourt, Brace & World, *Surprised by Joy* by C.S. Lewis, *Of Other Worlds* by C.S. Lewis, *Light on C.S. Lewis*, edited by Jocelyn Gibb, and *Poems* by C.S. Lewis, this last title being copyright ©1964 by the Executors of the Estate of C.S. Lewis, and reprinted by permission of Harcourt, Brace & World, Inc.

CONTENTS

Introduction

When I first wrote this little book, twenty years ago, I had read everything Lewis published and had enough notes for a book four times as long. But when I proposed the longer book to my original publisher, he replied, "We like your book, but we think Lewis' star has risen and is about to set. His day is over. No one will be reading C.S. Lewis twenty years from now."

So much for false prophets. Books on Lewis have multiplied like rabbits, or like flies around honey. The metaphor is insulting but almost apt, for though most of the many books on Lewis are honest and respectable pieces of work (the glaring exception is John Beverslius' abomination of desolation, *C.S. Lewis and the Search for Rational Religion*), most are not worth reading because they do little more than rehash what Lewis already said much, much more effectively than any of his summarizers and commentators can.

Indeed, I think it is a general truth that the more perfect the primary source, the duller and more worthless the secondary source. In my own field of philosophy this is almost always true: books on Socrates, Plato, Augustine, Pascal, James, and Kierkegaard (the most interesting philosophers and the ones with the best styles) are almost always dull and tedious, while books about Aristotle, Kant, Hegel, or Marx (dull philosophers with terrible styles) are often sprightly, challenging, and useful. The most glaring example of all is the Bible. The most exciting book ever written has spawned the dullest commentaries. So the dullness and the superfluity of the secondary sources on Lewis is one more testimony to his greatness.

Why read *this* book then? It has three distinctive features which most books on Lewis do not have. First, it does not summarize Lewis, but only introduces him to beginning students and readers, like a matchmaker. It is a salesman's sample. Second, it has the good sense to use Lewis' words rather than mine whenever possible. I think about half the word count in the book consists of quotations. Third, it is short.

If I were to rewrite this book today, I would amend at least one thing in addition to a few stylistic changes. I think I was too eager to be impartial and thus to find some fault with the writer whom I admire more than any other in this century. Teachers usually tend to take extra care to grade students they especially favor more severely, and students they disfavor more generously, to compensate for inevitable personal prejudice. I think I was too hard on *The Pilgrim's Regress* and *Dymer*, and also too concerned to place Lewis in the middle between the Left and the Right, bending over backwards to avoid labelling him a "conservative." Politically, this is essentially correct, as is clear from the passage on page 29 about what a truly Christian society would look like. But theologically and philosophically, Lewis clearly is the enemy of the Leftist, the Modernist, the revisionist. And even politically, he *is* a "conservative" in the European, Burkean sense of the word, if not the American.

The phenomenon of Lewis' continued popularity is easily explained. Just read him. "Come and see." You will find permeating all his writing qualities of excellence that function like fish hooks with which he catches you in the throat: joy, honesty, clarity, imagination, objectivity, orthodoxy, concreteness, analogies to common experience, brevity, wit—I cannot think of a single important desideratum for a writer that is missing. When anyone asks me, "How can I learn to write well?" I say, "Imitation. Read good writers. Start with C.S. Lewis."

More importantly, when they ask, "How can we learn to be good Christians in the modern world?" I refer them to the same man. And I frequently refer to him in my prayers, thanking God for His gift of the man who has helped save more people's intellectual and imaginative sanity and perhaps even souls than anyone else I know in this century. That is the essence of his greatness and his continuing appeal.

The Romantic Rationalist: Lewis the Man

Once upon a dreary era, when the World of Functional Specialization had nearly made obsolete all universal geniuses, romantic poets, Platonic idealists, rhetorical craftsmen, and even orthodox Christians, there appeared a man (almost as if from another world, one of the worlds of his own fiction: was he a man or something more like elf or angel?) who was all of these things as *amateur*, as well as probably the world's foremost authority in his professional province, medieval and Renaissance English literature. Before his death in 1963 he found time to produce some sixty first-quality works of literary history, literary criticism, theology, philosophy, autobiography, Biblical studies, historical philology, fantasy, science fiction, letters, poems, sermons, formal and informal essays, a historical novel, a spiritual diary, religious allegory, short stories, and children's novels. Clive Staples Lewis was not a man: he was a world.

His life is best told by himself. *Surprised by Joy* is a surprisingly objective autobiography — almost a *philosophy* of Joy — which he himself called "suffocatingly subjective": an indication of the remarkable lack of egotism of a mind which found nearly everything fascinating except itself. His biography is physically (though not spiritually) uneventful; but his personality is such a significantly anomalous event in the life of that already anomalous creature, Twentieth-Century Man, that we must investigate this man at length before investigating his works.

One way to approach a writer's personality is to note the major influences on his thought. For Lewis, these would include Plato, Augustine, Kant, English mystics such as Law and Temple, George MacDonald, William Morris, G.K. Chesterton, Owen Barfield, J.R.R. Tolkien, and Charles Williams (these last three, close personal friends); but he is acquainted on a first-name basis with the whole of Western man's history ("from the anthropoid to the agnostic") and cosmos ("from atoms to archangels"). Yet, so unpedantic that he seems unprofessional, he sits lightly on this immense inheritance, almost as if it were an indecency to bare his encyclopedic knowledge in any but his most technical writings.

Another way to summarize a man's personality is simply to list some of the things he likes; the thread binding these things together is usually intuited, even if not formulated. In one novel alone (*That Hideous Strength*) we find Lewis liking so many things that even a partial list constitutes an incredibly commodious cosmos: love, age, youth, joviality, seriousness, trivia, solitude, self-forgetfulness, maids, old maids, omens, runes, bright colors, femininity, masculinity, "the silly," "the normal," the bearing of pain, antivivisection, cool houses, democracy, monarchy, ancient and colorful clothing, outer space, uncontrolled birth, gardening, definitions, planets, romance, rules, humility, motherhood, the middle ages, honest skepticism, unmechanical things, beards, allegory, animals (especially tame bears and mice), God, woods, farmers, magic, punishment, friendship, ceremony, obedience (called "a dance"), hierarchy, weather, wonder, walking, organic life ("sweat, spittle, excretion"), classical education, vegetables, angels, belief in demons, the working class, honest anger, wine, patience, and riddles.

The binding thread must be a long one; perhaps the best way to formulate it is simply as a love of concrete *things*, both extraordinary ("splendid, remote, terrible, voluptuous, or celebrated things") and ordinary ("like flamingoes, German generals, lovers, sandwiches, pineapples, comets and kangaroos"). The universe is so rich, full, and fascinating to him that he feels no need to retreat into his own subjectivity: "we must not listen to Pope's maxim about the proper study of mankind. The proper study of man is everything." In a word, the key to Lewis's mind is its objectivity, its outer-directedness.

Objectivity is the key not only to his psychology but also to each genre of his works. Lewis's poetry and literary history and criticism may be used in illustration here, since this short essay prohibits extended comments on these genres. Lewis knew his poetry was too "naive" to be fashionable. The credo of his poetic program, as well as a typical example of it, is the first poem in the book:

A Confession

I am so coarse, the things the poets see
Are obstinately invisible to me.
For twenty years I've stared my level best
To see if evening — any evening — would suggest
A patient etherized upon a table;
In vain. I simply wasn't able.
To me each evening looked far more
Like the departure from a silent, yet a crowded, shore
Of a ship whose freight was everything, leaving behind
Gracefully, finally, without farewells, marooned mankind....

I'm like that odd man Wordsworth knew, to whom
A primrose was a yellow primrose, one whose doom
Keeps him forever in the list of dunces,
Compelled to live on stock responses,
Making the poor best that I can
Of dull things . . . peacocks, honey, the Great Wall, Aldebaran,
Silver weirs, new-cut grass, wave on the beach, hard gem,
The shapes of horse and woman, Athens, Troy, Jerusalem.

Objectivity is also the key to Lewis's literary history and criticism. "The first demand any work of art makes of us is surrender. Look. Listen. Receive. Get yourself out of the way. There is no good asking first whether the work before you deserves such a surrender, for until you have surrendered you cannot possibly find out" (*An Experiment in Criticism*).

Lewis counsels openness and emptiness because his universe is a *plenum*, a fullness. Some specifications must be made, though; certain themes stand out. The subtitle to *Pilgrim's*

Regress, an obscure and uncharitable post-conversion manifesto which Lewis accurately labels his worst book, nevertheless reveals his literary, philosophical and personal proclivities nicely at one fell swoop: "An Allegorical Apology for Christianity, Reason, and Romanticism." Lewis is, of all things, a romantic rationalist; and Christianity, he would insist, is the catalyst which allows these two diverse elements to combine in the compound of a single soul. Since these three themes constitute most of the man and most of his work, we must study each in some detail. First, the romantic; for of the three, Lewis himself insists that "the imaginative man in me is older, more continuously operative, and in that sense more basic than either the religious writer or the critic."

Lewis's romanticism centers around an experience he calls "Joy." He treats Joy on two levels: first a psychological description, then a religious interpretation. The introduction to *Pilgrim's Regress* first describes the experience as

> one of intense longing. It is distinguished from other longings by two things. In the first place, though the sense of want is acute and even painful, yet the mere wanting is felt to be somehow a delight. . . . In the second place, there is a peculiar mystery about the *object* of this Desire. . . . every one of those supposed objects for the Desire is inadequate to it.

The religious interpretation follows:

> It appeared to me therefore that if a man diligently followed this desire, pursuing the false objects until their falsity appeared and then resolutely abandoning them, he must come out at last into the clear knowledge that the human soul was made to enjoy some object that is never fully given — nay, cannot even be imagined as given — in our present mode of subjective and spatio-temporal experience. This Desire was in the soul as the Siege Perilous in Arthur's castle — the chair in which only one could sit. (*Pilgrim's Regress*)

It is almost as if Lewis had received a transplant of Augustine's "restless heart"; and it is a good summary of his own spiritual autobiography.

Lewis's chapter on Heaven in *The Problem of Pain* puts the experience into such enticing language that lengthy quotation becomes a necessity:

> You may have noticed that the books you really love are bound together by a secret thread. You know very well what is the common quality that makes you love them, though you cannot put it into words; but most of your friends do not see it at all, and often wonder why, liking this, you would also like that. Again, you have often stood before some landscape, which seems to embody what you have been looking for all your life; and then turned to the friend at your side who appears to be seeing what you saw — but at the first words a gulf yawns between you, and you realise that this sandscape means something totally different to him, that he is pursuing an alien vision and cares nothing for the ineffable suggestion by which you are transported. Even in your hobbies, has there not always been some secret attraction which the others are curiously ignorant of — something, not to be identified with, but always on the verge of breaking through, the smell of cut wood in the workshop or the clap-clap of water against the boat's side? Are not all lifelong friendships born at the moment when at last you meet another human being who has some inkling (but faint and uncertain even in the best) of that something which you were born desiring, and which, beneath the flux of other desires and in all the momentary silences between the louder passions, night and day, year by year, from childhood to old age, you are looking for, watching for, listening for? You have never *had* it. All the things that have ever deeply possessed your soul have been but hints of it — tantalising glimpses, promises never quite fulfilled, echoes that died away just as they caught your ear. But if it should really become manifest — if there ever came an echo that did not die away but swelled into the sound itself — you would know it. Beyond all possibility of doubt you would say "Here at last is the thing I was made for." We cannot tell each other about it. It is the secret signature of each soul, the

incommunicable and unappeasable want, the thing we
desired before we met our wives or made our friends or
chose our work, and which we shall still desire on our
deathbeds, when the mind no longer knows wife or friend or
work. While we are, this is. If we lose this, we lose all.

Lewis's religious solution to this psychological puzzle is even
more moving than the puzzle itself:

Your soul has a curious shape because it is a hollow made to
fit a particular swelling in the infinite contours of the divine
substance, or a key to unlock one of the doors in the house
with many mansions. Each of the redeemed shall forever
know and praise some one aspect of the divine beauty
better than any other creature can. Why else were
individuals created, but that God, loving each infinitely,
should love each differently? . . . For doubtless the
continually successful, yet never completed, attempt by each
soul to communicate its unique vision to all others (and that
by means whereof earthly art and philosophy are but clumsy
imitations) is also among the ends for which the individual
was created. . . . All your life an unattainable ecstasy has
hovered just beyond the grasp of your consciousness. The
day is coming when you will wake to find, beyond all hope,
that you have attained it, or else, that it was within your
reach and you have lost it forever. (*The Problem of Pain*)

If those who have had such an experience are few, those
who have felt it so deeply fewer, and those who have not only felt
it so deeply fewer, and those who have not only felt it but also
expressed it so movingly fewer still, those who have had a rational
string to their bow as well, and one as strong as this romantic
string, are practically nonexistent. (Lewis, however, is *not*
practically nonexistent!) He traces his rationalism to his tutor,
Kirk ("the Great Knock"). It is easy to see why he does from his
account of their first meeting:

I began to 'make conversation' in the deplorable
manner which I had acquired at those evening parties. . . . I

said I was surprised at the 'scenery' of Surrey; it was much 'wilder' than I had Expected.

"Stop!" shouted Kirk with a suddenness that made me jump. "What do you mean by wildness and what grounds had you for not expecting it?"

I replied I don't know what, still 'making conversation.' As answer after answer was torn to shreds it at last dawned upon me that he really wanted to know. He was not making conversation, nor joking, nor snubbing me; he wanted to know. I was stunned into attempting a real answer. A few passes sufficed to show that I had no clear and distinct idea corresponding to the word 'wildness,' and that, in so far as I had any idea at all, 'wildness' was a singularly inept word. "Do you not see, then," concluded the Great Knock, "that your remark was meaningless?" I prepared to sulk a little, assuming that the subject would now be dropped. Never was I more mistaken in my life. Having analyzed my terms, Kirk was proceeding to deal with my proposition as a whole. On what had I based (but he pronounced it *baized*) my expectations about the flora and geology of Surrey? Was it maps, or photographs, or books? I could produce none. It had, heaven help me, never occurred to me that what I called my thoughts needed to be "baized" on anything. . . .

If ever a man came near to being a purely logical entity, that man was Kirk. Born a little later, he would have been a Logical Positivist. The idea that human beings should exercise their vocal organs for any purpose except that of communicating or discovering truth was to him preposterous. (*Surprised by Joy*)

The romantic-rational blend was far from automatic. A catalyst was needed, powerful enough to make peace between two very diverse powers. Before his conversion to Christianity, he confessed,

the two hemispheres of my mind were in the sharpest contrast. On the one side a many-islanded sea of poetry and myth; on the other a glib and shallow 'rationalism.' Nearly

> all that I loved I believed to be imaginary; nearly all that I
> believed to be real I thought grim and meaningless. (*Ibid.*)

The union, far from compromising both components, heightened them: the romanticism of his later mythic fiction, both adult and children's, is incomparably more mature, intelligible, and philosophically profound than that of *Dymer*, his first publication, a tedious and obscure romantic poem; and the dialectical skill and theological bull's-eye hitting of his later apologetics put the wooden technique and small-minded name-calling of *Pilgrim's Regress* to shame. Both his romantic maturity and his rational maturity flow from his Christian maturity.

A writer's personality is often as evident in his style as in his content; and here too Lewis is both rationalist and romantic. A lucid style seems to be a nearly automatic result of an English classical education such as Lewis's, in which "to figure out the meaning of a sentence from Cicero is not too great an intellectual feat, but to put it into English that sounds like English is so severe a discipline that original composition in the native tongue henceforth seems a pleasant recreation" (*ibid.*). Lewis has the typically British stylistic excellence which combines the best of Anglo-Saxon (clarity, simplicity, directness, strong, rock-hard nouns and bright, arrow-like verbs) with the best of Latin (logic, balance, elegance, harmonious structure) in a synthesis of economy, precision, and deceptive ease. But there is love as well as lucidity and balance in Lewis's words. In fact, even in his philology he is a romantic: *Studies in Words* is not only immensely scholarly but also immensely "sympathetic" with words. Once again it is one of his tutors who is largely responsible, the one described in these lines: "Of Milton's 'Thrones, Dominations, Princedoms, Virtues, Powers,' he said, 'That line made me happy for a week.' It was not the sort of thing I had heard anyone say before"(*ibid.*).

One thing that makes Lewis's style of Christianity so appealing is his style of expression: both are concrete, vivid, empty of "gas" and full of solid stuff. Instead of saying "we must be spiritually regenerated" he says "We're like eggs at present. And you can't go on indefinitely being just an ordinary, decent egg. We must be hatched or go bad" (*Mere Christianity*). Theological profundity is often masked by simplicity of expression; for example: "while in other sciences the instruments you use are things external to yourself (things like microscopes and telescopes), the instrument through which you see God is your whole self" (*ibid.*). Lewis's stylistic simplicity can make even the obscurest of dogmas intelligible and relevant to ordinary experience. Here is the Trinity in three sentences:

> God is the thing to which he is praying — the goal which he is trying to reach. God is also the thing inside him which is pushing him on — the motive power. God is also the road or bridge along which he is being pushed to that goal. So that the whole threefold life of the three-personal Being is actually going on in that ordinary little bedroom where an ordinary man is saying his prayers.(*ibid.*)

Lewis knows that one metaphor can say more than tomes of abstraction; for example, on individuality and the Church he says:

> Things which are parts of a single organism may be very different from one another: things which are not, may be very alike. Six pennies are quite separate and very alike; my nose and my lungs are very different but they are only alive at all because they are parts of my body and share in its common life. Christianity thinks of human individuals not as mere members in a group or items in a list, but as organs in a body — different from one another and each contributing what no other could.(*ibid.*)

Lewis has taken Chesterton's stylistic advice:

> If you say 'The social utility of the indeterminate sentence is recognized by all criminologists as a part of our sociological evolution towards a more humane and scientific view of punishment,' you can go on talking like that for hours with hardly a movement of the gray matter inside your skull. But

> if you begin 'I wish Jones to go to gaol and Brown to say
> when Jones shall come out,' you will discover, with a thrill of
> horror, that you are obliged to think. (*Orthodoxy*)

Lewis alienates many readers by the same quality that wins
others: simple honesty. "His approach is so direct that many
authorities on winning friends and influencing people would
advise against it," notes Chad Walsh. In fact, one of my students
ritualistically throws shoes at *The Problem of Pain*, and another
refuses "to live in the same world with that man." (I do not know
whether he contemplates a pact with the Devil or a lunar landing
as an alternative.) Here are two key examples of unpopularly
honest approaches to unpopular doctrines:

> We are very shy nowadays of even mentioning heaven. We
> are afraid of the jeer about 'pie in the sky,' and of being told
> that we are trying to 'escape' from the duty of making a
> happy world here and now into dreams of a happy world
> elsewhere. But either there is 'pie in the sky' or there is not.
> If there is not, then Christianity is false, for this doctrine is
> woven into its whole fabric. If there is, then this truth, like
> any other, must be faced, whether it is useful at political
> meetings or no. (*The Problem of Pain*)

> The accounts of the 'miracles' in first century Palestine are
> either lies, or legends, or history. And if all, or the most
> important, of them are lies or legends, then the claim which
> Christianity has been making for the last two thousand years
> is simply false. No doubt it might even so contain noble
> sentiments and moral truths. So does Greek mythology; so
> does Norse. But that is a quite different affair. (*Miracles*)

The wit, too, of Lewis's apologetic style can offend as well as
attract. Though he evidently enjoys cutting through the fuzzy
thinking of fashionable axioms, his satiric sword is usually
sheathed, for he is more concerned with telling truths than with
refuting lies. But in that scabbard is a sharp blade. Consider this
exchange in *Pilgrim's Regress*:

'But how do you *know* there is no Landlord?'

'Christopher Columbus, Galileo, the earth is round, invention of printing, gunpowder!' exclaimed Mr. Enlightenment in such a loud voice that the pony shied.

'I beg your pardon,' said John.

'Eh?' said Mr. Enlightenment.

'I don't quite understand,' said John.

'Why, it's as plain as a pikestaff,' said the other. 'Your people in Puritania believe in the Landlord because they have not had the benefits of a scientific training. For example, now, I dare say it would be news to you to hear that the earthwas round — round as an orange, my lad!'

'Well, I don't know that it would,' said John, feeling a little disappointed. 'My father always said it was round.'

'No, no, my dear boy,' said Mr. Enlightenment, 'you must have misunderstood him. It is well known that everyone in Puritania thinks the earth flat. It is not likely that I should be mistaken on such a point. Indeed, it is out of the question. Then again, there is the palaeontological evidence.'

'What's that?'

'Why, they tell you in Puritania that the Landlord made all these roads. But that is quite impossible for old people can remember the time when the roads were not nearly so good as they are now. and what is more, scientists have found all over the country the traces of *old* roads running in quite different directions. The inference is obvious.'

John said nothing.

'I said,' repeated Mr. Enlightenment, 'that the inference was obvious.'

'Oh, yes, yes, of course,' said John hastily, turning a little red.

More often, the wit is harmless and pleasant:

I have been warned not even to raise the question of animal immortality, lest I find myself 'in company with all the old maids.' I have no objection to the company. I do not think either virginity or old age contemptible. . . . Nor am I greatly moved by jocular enquiries such as 'Where will you put all the mosquitoes?' — a question to be answered on its own level by pointing out that, if the worst came to the worst, a heaven for mosquitoes and a hell for men could very conveniently be combined. (*The Problem of Pain*)

But it is honesty that triumphs over wit. He uses his wit so sparingly as to seem embarrassed by it, but his honesty is ubiquitous, compelling even admissions of dishonesty (just as humility means admitting we are proud). He writes to Dorothy Sayers that "a doctrine never seems dimmer to me than when I have just successfully defended it," and he repents the winning of right battles with wrong weapons in "The Apologist's Evening Prayer":

> From all my lame defeats and oh! much more
> From all the victories that I seemed to score;
> From cleverness shot forth on Thy behalf
> At which, while angles weep, the audience laugh;
> From all my proofs of Thy divinity,
> Thou, who wouldst give no sign, deliver me.
>
> Thoughts are but coins. Let me not trust, instead
> Of Thee, their thin-worn image of Thy head.
> From all my thoughts, even from my thoughts of Thee,
> O thou fair Silence, fall, and set me free.
> Lord of the narrow gate and the needle's eye,
> Take from me all my trumpery lest I die.

The Funeral of A Great Myth:
Lewis's Attack on Modernity

The three main strings to Lewis's bow, Rationalism, Romanticism and Christianity, correspond to the three main genres of his writing, literary criticism, imaginative fiction and apologetics. All three genres carry the common theme of a "lover's quarrel with the world" of modernity. Before considering the three separately, we should consider this common theme; for it is the main source of Lewis's historical significance.

Few men (and fewer Christians) have had as frank, as fresh, and as pagan a love of the world; yet few men (and fewer modern men) have had as frank, as fresh, and as Christian an animus against the world which he describes in terms like these:

> However far you went you would find the machines, the crowded cities, the empty thrones, the false writings, the barren beds; men maddened with false promises and soured with true miseries, worshiping the iron works of their own hands, cut off from Earth their mother and from the Father in Heaven. . . . The shadow of one dark wing is over all Tellus. (*That Hideous Strength*)

> Their labour-saving devices multiply drudgery; their aphrodisiacs make them impotent; their amusements bore them; their rapid production of food leaves half of them starving, and their devices for saving time have banished leisure from their country. (*Pilgrim's Regress*)

What could cause a man who was more a wondering child than a fusty old grump to play the prophet Amos against the modern world?

One reason, which makes him at least unafraid to do so, is his honesty. He does not care what is new, only what is true. In *Surprised by Joy* he relates how Owen Barfield

> made short work of what I have called my 'chronological snobbery,' the uncritical assumption that whatever has gone out of date is on that account discredited. You must find why it went out of date. Was it ever refuted (and if so by whom, where, and how conclusively) [shades of the Great Knock!] or did it merely die away as fashions do? If the latter, this tells us nothing about its truth or falsehood. From seeing this, one passes to the realization that our own age is also 'a period,' and certainly has, like all periods, its own characteristic illusions. They are likeliest to lurk in those widespread assumptions which are so ingrained in the age that no one dares to attack or feels it necessary to defend them.

If this first reason allows Lewis's dissent from modernity, a second requires it: modernity's own "chronological snobbery." A man so thoroughly acquainted with "the data of greatness" that his colleagues never ceased to marvel at the ubiquitous glint of recognition in his eyes whenever anyone quoted a line of classical, medieval, or Renaissance literature, could hardly be expected to hold his patience at the cavalier dismissal of the past as one great foible, or even as a mere lower rung on the evolutionary ladder.   Lewis sees modernity from a longer perspectIve, and he does not like what he sees: our "idolizing as the goddess History what manlier ages belaboured as the strumpet Fortune" and our forgetting that "humanity does not pass through phases as a train passes through stations. . . . whatever we have been, in some sort we are still."

The third and most substantial reason for Lewis's anti-modern polemic is his reasoned disagreement with the basic cosmological model of most modern thought, the presupposed "background world" thought more *in terms of* than thought *about* — like eyeglasses looked through but not looked at. this axiom is Universal Evolutionism, and Lewis offers it a respectful but conclusive burial in the essay "The Funeral of a Great Myth" and throughout his writings. Examination of his polemic is central not only to the understanding of Lewis but also to the evaluation of modernity.

Lewis's major philosophical argument against the myth is that it contains a self-contradiction:

> The Myth asks me to believe that reason is simply the unforeseen and unintended by-product of a mindless process at one stage of its endless and aimless becoming. The content of the Myth thus knocks out from under me the only ground on which I could possibly believe the Myth to be true. If my own mind is a product of the irrational — if what seem my clearest reasonings are only the way in which a creature conditioned as I am is bound to feel — how shall I trust my mind when it tells me about Evolution? ("The Funeral of a Great Myth")

The Myth is not, in fact, accepted on rational grounds, Lewis thinks, but by a kind of conditioning:

> If popular Evolutionism were (as it imagines itself to be) not a Myth but the intellectually legitimate result of the scientific theorem on the public mind, it would arise *after* that theorem had become widely known. . . . In fact, however, we find something quite different. The clearest and finest poetical expressions of the Myth come before the *Origin of Species* was published (1859) and long before it had established itself as scientific orthodoxy. . . . in Keats' *Hyperion* and Wagner's *Ring*. (*Ibid.*)

> If water stands too long it stinks. To infer thence that whatever stands long must be unwholesome is to be the victim of metaphor. . . . The square on the hypotenuse has not gone mouldy by continuing to equal the sum of the squares on the other two sides. ("The Poison of Subjectivism")

> I submit that what has imposed this climate of opinion so firmly on the human mind is a new archetypal image. It is the image of old machines being superseded by new and

better ones. For in the world of machines the new most
often really is better and the primitive really is clumsy. ("De
Descriptione Temporum")

What philosophy of history does Lewis substitute for the
evolutionary one in his own historical studies? None!

> About everything that could be called 'the philosophy of
> history' I am a desperate skeptic. I know nothing of the
> future, not even whether there will be any future. . . . I don't
> know whether the human tragi-comedy is now in Act I or
> Act V, whether our present disorders are those of infancy or
> old age. (*Ibid.*)

> Some think it the historian's business to penetrate beyond
> this apparent confusion and heterogeneity, and to grasp in a
> simple intuition the 'spirit' or 'meaning' of his period. With
> some hesitation, and with much respect for the great men
> who have thought otherwise, I submit that this is exactly
> what we must refrain from doing. I cannot convince myself
> that such 'spirits' or 'meanings' have much more reality than
> the pictures we see in the fire. . . . The 'canals' on Mars
> vanished when we got stronger lenses. [And any reader of
> *The Sixteenth Century* or *The Discarded Image* knows that
> Lewis has strong lenses!] (*History of English Literature in the
> Sixteenth Century Excluding Drama*)

> Between different ages there is no impartial judge on earth,
> for no one stands outside the historical process; and of
> course no one is so completely enslaved to it as those who
> take our own age to be, not one more period, but a final and
> permanent platform from which we can see all other ages
> objectively. (*Reflections on the Psalms*)

What is left then for the historian to do? Some idea can be
gotten from Lewis's own practice. He presents the mind of
another age in its own terms, with such empathy and
understanding that the reader knows he is presenting a part of
himself, not an alien object. One typical example from *The
Discarded Image*:

Every boy, out of school, without noticing it, then acquired a
range of knowledge. . . . (including) farriery, forestry,
archery, hawking, sowing, dichting, thatching, brewing,
baking, weaving, and practical astronomy. This concrete
knowledge mixed with their law, rhetoric, theology, and
mythology, bred an outlook very different from our own.
High abstractions and rarefied artifices jostled the earthiest
particulars. They would have found it very hard to
understand the modern educated man who, though
'interested in astronomy,' knows neither who the Pleiades
were nor where to look for them in the sky. They talked
more readily than we about large universals such as death,
change, fortune, friendship, or salvation; but also about pigs,
loaves, boots, and boats. The mind darted more easily to
and fro between that mental heaven and earth: the cloud of
middle generalizations, hanging between the two, was then
much smaller. . . . they talk something like angels and
something like sailors and stableboys; never like civil
servants or writers of leading articles.

Lewis does not counsel *return* to the medieval model, but *respect*
for it:

I am only suggesting considerations that may induce us to
regard all models in the right way, respecting each and
idolising none. We can no longer dismiss the change of
Models as a simple progress from error to truth. No Model
is a catalogue of ultimate realities, and none is a mere
fantasy. . . . each reflects the prevalent psychology of an age
almost as much as it reflects the state of that age's
knowledge. Hardly any battery of new facts could have
persuaded a Greek that the universe had an attribute so
repugnant to him as infinity; hardly any such battery could
persuade a modern that is hierarchical. (*The Discarded
Image*)

Lewis himself comes close to a philosophy of history in
locating the essential change from medieval to modern man as
one of subjectivization,

that great movement of internalization and that consequent
aggrandizement of man and dessication of the outer

universe in which the psychological history of the West has
so largely consisted. . . . man with his new powers became
rich like Midas but all that he touched had gone dead and
cold. (*Ibid.*)

The result is the present situation of a bare, isolated ego
and a mathematical, valueless universe in naked confrontation.
Lewis plunges one more step into the philosophy of history in
hopefully interpreting the present crisis as adolescence, not
senility: the doubting which turns a child's faith in authority to
an adult's experiential conviction:

It may be that the Power which rules our species is at this
moment carrying out a daring experiment. Could it be
intended that the whole mass of the people should now
move forward and occupy for themselves those heights
which were once reserved for the sages? Is the distinction
between wise and simple to disappear because all are now
expected to become wise? If so, our present blunderings
would be but growing pains. (*Miracles*)

Mere Christianity:
Lewis's Religious Philosophy

Although Lewis's explicitly religious writings constitute only a part, and perhaps not even the greatest part, of his contribution to literature, this chapter, which considers his religious philosophy, will be the longest. For nearly every theme in his rather didactic fiction is also treated overtly in his religious and philosophical essays or his three major systematic books: *Miracles*, *The Problem of Pain* and *The Abolition of Man*. There is no need to read a "world and life view" into or out of Lewis's fiction: it stares us in the face in his essays and systematic books.

The content of this philosophy is, in a word, "mere Christianity." The meaning of the term is clear from the preface to the famous wartime BBC broadcast talks collected under this title:

> There is no mystery about my own position. I am a very ordinary layman of the Church of England, not especially 'high,' nor especially 'low,' nor especially anything else. But in this book I am not trying to convert anyone to my own position. Ever since I became a Christian I have thought that the best, perhaps the only service I could do for my unbelieving neighbours was to explain and defend the belief that has been common to nearly all Christians at all times.... what Baxter calls 'mere' Christianity.

What Lewis's unique personality adds to this traditional content is a blend of imagination, clarity, and honesty which I have labelled 'romanticism,' 'rationalism' and 'objectivity' respectively. And it is the third, I believe, that is the key to his mind and to his philosophy.

In its simplest sense, "objectivity" is the psychological attitude of interest in the object rather than in the subject. Lewis calls even emotions objective in this sense, for "we are not really concerned with the emotions; the emotions are our concern about something else." He observes (wisely) that psychological health demands that the primary object of our interest be something greater than ourselves:

> Even in social life, you will never make a good impression on other people until you stop thinking about what sort of impression you are making. Even in literature and art, no man who bothers about originality will ever be original: whereas if you simply try to tell the truth (without caring twopence how often it has been told before) you will, nine times out of ten, become original without ever having noticed it. [Surely this is the origin of Lewis's own great originality.] The principle runs through all life from top to bottom. Give up your self and you will find your real self. (*Mere Christianity*)

The same principle applies to religion. Lewis is convinced from experience that

> in deepest solitude there is a road right out of the self, a commerce with something which, by refusing to identify itself with any object of the senses, or anything whereof we have biological or social need, or anything imagined, or any state of our own minds, proclaims itself sheerly objective. Far more objective than bodies, for it is not, like them, clothed in our senses; the naked other, imageless (though our imagination salutes it with a hundred images), unknown, undefined, desired. (*Surprised by Joy*)

And adored, adored with a "quite disinterested self-abandonment to an object which securely claimed this simply by being the object it was." For "a thing can be revered not for what it can do to us but for what it is in itself." As Chesterton says, one of man's most pragmatic needs is to be something more than a pragmatist.

The attitude of objectivity delivers us from the onerous, divine task of *creating* meaning out of our own subjectivity, into the humbler and more cheerful, human task of *discovering* it. As a consequence, there is enough "margin" to life, enough "world-space," enough "spiritual room" for relaxation, wonder, and play. The contemplative can enjoy the world because he loses himself in it, thus paradoxically finding himself as well as the world; the activist tries to conquer the world and loses it in himself, thus finding neither his real self nor the real world. In other words, we can possess the universe only by renouncing possession; it reveals its beauty to us only if we let it be itself, gloriously independent of us. As the planetary eldils tell Ransom in *Perelandra,*

> Though men or angels rule them, the worlds are for themselves. The waters you have not floated on, the fruit you have not plucked, the caves into which you have not descended and the fire through which your bodies cannot pass, do not await your coming to put on perfection, though they will obey you when you come. Times without number I have circled Arbol while you were not alive, and those times were not desert. Their own voice was in them, not merely a dreaming of the day when you should awake. They also were at the centre. . . . Where Maleldil is, there is the centre. He is in every place. . . . Be comforted, small immortals. You are not the voice that all things utter, nor is there eternal silence in the places where you cannot come. No feet have walked, nor shall, on the ice of Glund; no eye looked up from beneath on the Ring of Lurga, and Ironplain in Neruval is chaste and empty. Yet it is not for nothing that the gods walk ceaselessly around the fields of Arbol. Blessed be He!

"Objectivity" is more than a psychological attitude for Lewis: it is also a philosophy of human knowledge:

> Perhaps the safest way of putting it is this: that we must give up talking about 'human reason'. . . . Where thought is strictly rational it must be, in some odd sense, not ours, but cosmic or super-cosmic. It must be something not shut up

inside our heads but already 'out there' — in the universe or behind the universe: either as objective as material Nature or more objective still. Unless all that we take to be knowledge is an illusion, we must hold that in thinking we are not reading rationality into an irrational universe but responding to a rationality with which the universe has always been saturated. . . . For if our minds are totally alien to reality then all our thoughts, including this thought, are worthless. We must, then, grant logic to reality; we must, if we are to have any moral standards, grant it moral standards too. And there is really no reason why we should not do the same about standards of beauty. ("De Futilitate")

Finally, "objectivity" is not only a psychology and an epistemology but also a cosmology; and the cosmos it reveals is one in which there are more, not fewer, things in heaven and earth than are dreamed of in our philosophies. The object of Lewis's constant polemic is the reductionist, "the trousered ape who has never been able to conceive the Atlantic as anything but so many million tons of cold salt water."

The strength of such a [reductionist] critic lies in the words 'merely' or 'nothing but.' He sees all the facts but not the meaning. Quite truly, therefore, he claims to have seen all the facts. There *is* nothing else there; except the meaning. He is, therefore, as regards the matter in hand, in the position of an animal. You will have noticed that most dogs cannot understand *pointing*. You point to a bit of food on the floor: the dog, instead of looking at the floor, sniffs at your finger. A finger is a finger to him, and that is all. His world is all fact and no meaning. And in a period when factual realism is dominant we shall find people deliberately inducing upon themselves this dog-like mind. . . . There will always be evidence, and every month fresh evidence, to show that religion is only psychological, justice only self-protection, politics only economics, love only lust, and thought itself only cerebral biochemistry. ("Transposition")

[But] you cannot go on 'seeing through' things for ever. The whole point of seeing through something is to see something through it. It is good that the window should be transparent,

because the street or garden beyond it is opaque. How if
you saw through the garden too? . . . If you see through
everything, then everything is transparent. But a wholly
transparent world is an invisible world. To 'see through' all
things is the same as not to see. (*The Abolition of Man*)

We should never ask of anything 'Is it real?' for everything is
real. The proper question is, 'A real *what?*' (*Letters to
Malcolm: Chiefly on Prayer*)

The role of Christian apologist is an unpopular one today
not primarily because of the unpopularity of Christianity but
because of the unpopularity of apologetics. Lewis avoids the
apologetic Scylla and Charybdis by his simple, rational
objectivity. He is neither the arrogant, militaristic inquisitor nor
the embarrassed apologizer who seems to believe less in his own
product than in others. He shares neither past Christendom's
superiority complex nor present Christendom's inferiority
complex. And he does this by asking simply "is it true?" not "is it
new?"

What makes some theological works like sawdust to me is
the way the authors can go on discussing how far certain
positions are adjustable to contemporary thought, or
beneficial in relation to social problems, or 'have a future'
before them, but never squarely ask what grounds we have
for supposing them to be true accounts of any objective
reality. As if we were trying to make rather than to learn.
Have we no Other to reckon with? (*Ibid.*)

Since Lewis dares to be a "Christian rationalist," we can
anticipate his giving reasons for his faith. These reasons are not
rationalizations, that is, reasons sought out only to convince
others of something he himself accepted for quite different
reasons. For he confesses: "I'm not the religious type. I want to
be left alone, to feel I'm my own master; but since the facts
seemed to be the opposite I had to give in" (*ibid.*). He gave in
"kicking and struggling," "the most reluctant convert in all of

England." The rationalism he preaches is only the rationalism he practices.

Lewis's apologetic pares down to one central argument for Christianity, one road into the City of God from which all other streets branch out, one front-door key that unlocks the whole house of many mansions. It is the central claim of Christianity the claim of Christ to be God:

> The claim is so shocking — a paradox, and even a horror, which we may easily be lulled into taking too lightly — that only two views of this man are possible. Either he was a raving lunatic of an unusually abominable type, or else He was, and is, precisely what He said. There is no middle way. If the records make the first hypothesis unacceptable, you must submit to the second. And if you do that, all else that is claimed by Christians becomes credible. (*The Problem of Pain*)

> One part of the claim tends to slip past us unnoticed because we have heard it so often that we no longer see what it amounts to. I mean the claim to forgive sins: any sins. Now unless the speaker is God, this is really so preposterous as to be comic. We can all understand how a man forgives offences against himself. You tread on my toe and I forgive you, you steal my money and I forgive you. But what should we make of a man, himself unrobbed and untrodden on, who announced that he forgave you for treading on other men's toes and stealing other men's money? Asinine fatuity is the kindest description we should give of his conduct. Yet this is what Jesus did. . . . In the mouth of any speaker who is not God, these words would imply what I can only regard as a silliness and conceit unrivalled by any other character in history. Yet (and this is the strange, significant thing) even His enemies, when they read the Gospels, do not usually get the impression of silliness and conceit. Still less do unprejudiced readers.

> I am trying here to prevent anyone saying the really foolish thing that people often say about Him: "I'm ready to accept Jesus as a great moral teacher, but I don't accept His claim to be God." That is the one thing we must not say. A man

who was merely a man and said the sort of things Jesus said
would not be a great moral teacher. He would either be a
lunatic — on a level with the man who says he is a poached
egg — or else he would be the Devil of Hell. (*Mere
Christianity*)

This kind of orthodox Christian apologetic is usually
dismissed with that catch-all of contemporary invective,
"conservative." The labelling is, of course, far too simple. "The
hobgoblin of little minds" is not consistency but oversimplified
categorization; and the least thought-taxing categories of a
politically conscious and politically changing age are "liberal" and
"conservative" (often only pretentious polysyllabications for
"new" and "old"). Lewis stands out above such categories, like
most stand-out Christians of his or any age. For Lewis is neither
a Christian conservative nor a Christian radical, but a radical
Christian. His "mere Christianity" is radical for the same reason
it is orthodox: it returns to its root (*radix*) rather than putting
forth new branches. If "conservative" means safe or dull, Lewis's
"mere Christianity" is not conservative but daring: it is what
Chesterton calls "the romance of orthodoxy."

The term "conservative" properly belongs to politics, and its
use elsewhere is analogical (an analogy usually carried far
beyond its limits). Can Lewis be called conservative in the
proper sense?

He is no political expert, and knows it, so the question is of
little importance, except as it relates to his apologetics. The
answer must be No. His most systematic statement on the
relation between Christianity and modern "one-two" ("right-left")
politics is the following:

> Christianity has not, and does not profess to have, a detailed
> political programme. . . . all the same, the New Testament,
> without going into details, gives us a pretty clear hint of what
> a fully Christian society would be like. Perhaps it gives us
> more than we can take. . . . If there were such a society in
> existence and you or I visited it, I think we should come

away with a curious impression. We should feel that its
economic life was very socialistic, and, in that sense,
'advanced,' but that its family life and its code of manners
were rather old-fashioned — perhaps even ceremonious
and aristocratic. Each of us would like some bits of it, but I
am afraid very few of us would like the whole thing. That is
just what one would expect if Christianity is the total plan
for the human machine. We have all departed from that
total plan in different ways, and each of us wants to make
out that his own modification of the original plan is the plan
itself. you will find this again and again about anything that
is really Christian: every one is attracted by bits of it and
wants to pick out those bits and leave the rest. . . . *A clear
knowledge of these truisms would be fatal both to the political
Left and to the political Right of modern times.* [Italics mine.]
(*Ibid.*)

Lewis has been called conservative or reactionary also
because of his attitude toward Science (especially by those who
capitalize the S). Clyde Kilby notes that "some are convinced
that Lewis is subconsciously afraid of science because it tends to
destroy what they call his theological dogmatism" (*The Christian
World of C.S. Lewis*). This charge, of course, is as unverifiable an
ad hominem as the reply that the critic is subconsciously afraid of
religion because of his scientific dogmatism! The "anti-scientific"
charge is made mainly on the basis of two books: a *Brave New
World*-like novel, *That Hideous Strength*, and *The Abolition of
Man*, which makes the point of the novel systematically. I shall
let the reader judge for himself the justice of the charge by simply
quoting the three key passages in *The Abolition of Man* on which
the charge is based:

There is something which unites magic and applied science
while separating both from the 'wisdom' of earlier ages. For
the wise men of old the cardinal problem had been how to
conform the soul to reality, and the solution had been
knowledge, self-discipline, and virtue. For magic and
applied science alike the problem is how to subdue reality to
the wishes of men: the solution is a technique.

What we call Man's power over Nature turns out to be a power exercised by some men over other men with Nature as its instrument. . . . The final stage is come when Man by eugenics, by pre-natal conditioning, and by an education and propaganda based on a perfect applied psychology, has obtained full control over himself. Human nature will be the last part of Nature to surrender to Man. . . . [but] they [the conditioned men] are not men at all: they are artifacts. Man's final conquest has proved to be the abolition of Man.

Nothing I can say will prevent some people from describing this lecture as an attack on science. I deny the charge, of course. . . . but I can go further than that. I even suggest that from Science herself the cure might come. . . . Is it possible to imagine a new Natural Philosophy, continually conscious that the 'natural object' produced by analysis and abstraction is not reality but only a view, and always correcting the abstraction? . . . The regenerate science which I have in mind would not do even to minerals and vegetables what modern science threatens to do to man himself. When it explained it would not explain away. . . . its followers would not be free with the words *only* and *merely*.

Lewis's "mere Christianity" is certainly not "conservative" but radical in its view of man, his dignity and his destiny:

It is a serious thing to live in a society of possible gods and goddesses, to remember that the dullest and most uninteresting person you can talk to may one day be a creature which, if you saw it now, you would be strongly tempted to worship, or else a horror and a corruption such as you now meet, if at all, only in a nightmare. All day long we are, in some degree, helping each other to one or other of these destinations. It is in the light of those overwhelming possibilities, it is with the awe and the circumspection proper to them, that we should conduct all our dealings with one another, all friEndships, all loves, all play, all politics. There are no *ordinary* people. You have never talked to a mere mortal. Nations, cultures, arts, civilisations — these are mortal, and their life is to ours as the life of a gnat. But it is immortals whom we joke with, work with, marry, snub,

and exploit — immortal horrors or everlasting splendours.
("The Weight of Glory")

Yet even more startling than this, "mere Christianity" offers us
the hope not merely of the immortality of the soul but of the
resurrection of the body; not merely the New Heaven but also the
New Earth:

> At this point awe and trembling fall upon us as we read the
> records. If the story is false, it is at least a much stranger
> story than we expected, something for which philosophical
> 'religion,' psychical research, and popular superstition have
> all alike failed to prepare us. If the story is true, then a
> wholly new mode of being has arisen in the universe. The
> body which lives in that new mode. . . . differently related to
> space and probably to time, but by no means cut off from all
> relation to them. . . . The picture is not what we expected. It
> is not the picture of an escape from any and every kind of
> Nature into some unconditioned and utterly transcendent
> life. It is the picture of a new human nature, and a new
> Nature in general, being brought into existence. . . . the old
> field of space, time, matter, and the senses is to be weeded,
> dug, and sown for a new crop. We may be tired of that old
> field; God is not. . . . It is useful to remember that even now
> senses responsive to different vibrations would admit us to
> quite new worlds of experience; that a multi-dimensional
> space would be different, almost beyond recognition, from
> the space we are now aware of, yet not discontinuous with it;
> that time may not always be for us, as it now is, unilinear
> and irreversible; that other parts of Nature might some day
> obey us as our cortex now does. . . . Spirit and Nature have
> quarreled in us; that is our disease. Nothing we can yet do
> enables us to imagine its complete healing. Some glimpses
> and faint hints we have: in the Sacraments, in the use made
> of sensuous imagery by the great poets, in the best instances
> of sexual love, in our experiences of the earth's beauty. But
> the full healing is utterly beyond our present conceptions.
> Mystics have got as far in the contemplation of God as the
> point at which the senses are banished: the further point, at
> which they will be put back again has (to the best of my
> knowledge) been reached by no one. . . . There is in our
> present pilgrim condition plenty of room (more room than

most of us like) for abstinence and renunciation and mortifying our natural desires. But behind all asceticism the thought should be, 'Who will trust us with the true wealth if we cannot be trusted even with the wealth that perishes? Who will trust me with a spiritual body if I cannot control even an earthly body?' These small and perishable bodies we now have were given to us as ponies are given to schoolboys. We must learn to manage: not that we may some day be free of horses altogether but that some day we may ride bare-back, confident and rejoicing, those greater mounts, those winged, shining and world-shaking horses which perhaps even now expect us with impatience, pawing and snorting in the King's stables. (*Miracles*)

Despite this radical hope, Lewis is often called a religious conservative because of the seriousness with which he takes traditional but currently unpopular doctrines like Heaven and Hell and the existence of the Devil. Some have suggested that it is Lewis's penchant for fantasy and a sort of inverted wish-fulfillment that draws him to these dogmas; others call it simply "a certain ill-concealed glee in adopting an old-fashioned and unpopular position" (this from Alan Watts in his provocative *Behold the Spirit*). It is neither: it is "objectivity." "Where we find a difficulty we may always expect that a discovery awaits us. Where there is cover we hope for game" (*Reflections on the Psalms*). Lewis seeks out rather than glossing over those aspects of the Christian claim which seem the most incredible, repellent, or surprising because he is open-minded enough to want to know, to want to modify rather than simply confirm his previous opinions. This is one reason many readers find him irksome. Everyone praises open-mindedness and willingness to revise opinions; but when a Lewis revises atheism to Christianity, pantheism to theism, and "Christianity-and-water" to "mere Christianity," and for highly objective reasons at that, his personality meanwhile "kicking and struggling," it is called wish-fulfillment and theological dogmatism! Open-mindedness often seems to be a one-way street.

The most unpopular doctrine in Christianity is certainly Hell. Though Lewis, like all sane men, finds Hell "detestable" and "intolerable" and confesses "I would pay any price to be able to say truthfully 'All will be saved,'" he finds it necessary to add:

> But my reason retorts, 'Without their will, or with it?' If I say, 'Without their will' I at once perceive a contradiction: how can the supreme voluntary act of self-surrender be involuntary? . . . If the happiness of a creature lies in self-surrender, no one can make that surrender but himself (though many can help him to make it) and he may refuse. . . . If I say 'With their will,' my reason replies 'How if they *will not* give in?' (*The Problem of Pain*)

There are, however, mitigations which make the doctrine almost tolerable. Though Christianity insists on the *existence* of Hell, we are free to construe its *nature* in far different terms than fire and brimstone:

> We are therefore at liberty — since the two conceptions, in the long run, mean the same thing — to think of this bad man's perdition not as a sentence imposed on him but as the mere fact of being what he is.

> You will remember that in the parable, the saved go to a place prepared for *them*, while the damned go to a place never made for men at all. To enter heaven is to become more human than you ever succeeded in being on earth; to enter hell, is to be banished from humanity. What is cast (or casts itself) into hell is not a man: it is 'remains.'

> The characteristic of lost souls is 'their rejection of everything that is not simply themselves.' Our imaginary egotist has tried to turn everything he meets into a province or appendage of the self. The taste for the *other*, that is, the very capacity for enjoying good, is quenched in him except in so far as his body still draws him into some rudimentary contact with an outer worlD. Death removes this last contact. He has his wish — to live wholly in the self and to make the best of what he finds there. And what he finds there is Hell. (*Ibid.*)

This is objectivity with a vengeance! The exact opposite of Sartre's "Hell is other people" is also a "No Exit"; a "no Other."

Perhaps such a Hell, though intolerable, is intelligible; but a Devil too? Since everyone seems to have read *The Screwtape Letters*, the question is bound to occur:

> 'Do you really mean at this time of day to re-introduce our old friend the devil — hoofs and horns and all?' Well, what the time of day has to do with it I do not know. And I am not particular about the hoofs and horns. (*Mere Christianity*)

> The doctrine of Satan's existence and fall is not among the things we know to be untrue: it contradicts not the facts discovered by scientists but the mere, vague 'climate of opinion' that we happen to be living in. Now I take a very low view of 'climates of opinion.' In his own subject every man knows that all discoveries are made and all errors corrected by those who ignore the 'climate of opinion.'

> If it offends you less, you may say that the 'life-force' is corrupted, where I say that living creatures were corrupted by an evil angelic being. We mean the same thing: but I find it easier to believe in a myth of gods and demons than in one of hypostatized abstract nouns. (*The Problem of Pain*)

The enormous antitheses of Heaven and Hell, God and Satan, are more, however, than the 'coin of the realm' of Lewis's world of myth and imagination, or even of his world of apologetics; they are "alarming and operative realities" to him. Paradoxically, it is the currently unattractive dogmas of "mere Christianity" that make his world, if not attractive, at least compelling, as Jane finds in *That Hideous Strength*:

> The vision of the universe which she had begun to see in the last few minutes had a curiously stormy quality about it. It was bright, darting, and overpowering. Old Testament imagery of eyes and wheels for the first time in her life took on some possibility of meaning. . . . If it had ever occurred to

her to question whether all these things might be the reality behind what she had been taught at school as 'religion,' she had put the thought aside. The distance between these alarming and operative realities and the memory, say, of fat Mrs. Dimble saying her prayers, was too wide. The things belonged, for her, to different worlds. On the one hand, terror of dreams, rapture of obedience, the tingling light and sound from under the Director's door, and the great struggle against an imminent danger; on the other, the smell of pews, horrible lithographs of the Savior (apparently seven feet high, with the face of a consumptive girl), the embarrassment of confirmation classes, the nervous affability of clergymen.

Heaven and Hell are not escapisms: they make earth more, not less important to Lewis. Life acquires a new profundity and its decisions an awesomeness:

We are not living in a world where all roads are radii of a circle and where all, if followed long enough, will therefore draw gradually nearer and finally meet at the centre; rather in a world where every road, after a few miles, forks into two, and each of those into two again, and at each fork you must make a decision. (*The Great Divorce*)

As there is one Face above all worlds merely to see which is irrevocable joy, so at the bottom of all worlds that face is waiting whose sight alone is the misery from which none who beholds it can recover. And though there seemed to be, and indeed were, a thousand roads by which a man could walk through the world, there was not a single one which did not lead sooner or later either to the Beatific or the Miserific Vision. . . . We walk every day on the razor edge between these two incredible possibilities. (*Perelandra*)

Strong meat this, and almost more dismaying than comforting.

I quite agree that the Christian religion is, in the long run, a thing of unspeakable comfort. But it does not begin in comfort; it begins in the dismay I have been describing, and it is no use at all trying to go on to that comfort without first going through that dismay. In religion, as in war and everything else, comfort is the one thing you cannot get by looking for it. If you look for truth, you may find comfort in the end: if you look for comfort you will not get either comfort or truth — only soft soap and wishful thinking to begin with and, in the end, despair. (*Mere Christianity*)

Lewis has also been labeled "conservative" because of his "moralism." He is a moral absolutist, and much of his anti-modern polemic is directed against moral relativism; for example, the *reductio ad absurdum* argument in *Miracles* which concludes: "If naturalism is true, 'I ought' is the same sort of statement as 'I itch'"; and his argument from self-contradiction against "the moral reformer who, after saying that 'good' means 'what We are conditioned to like' goes on cheerfully to consider whether it might be 'better' that we should be conditioned to like something else. What in Heaven's name does he mean by 'better'?" (*Letters*). Yet his absolutism covers the facts of cultural relativism too:

> A nation's moral outlook is just so much of its share in eternal Moral Wisdom as its history, economics, etc. lets through. In the same way the voice of the Announcer is just so much of a human voice as the receiving set lets through. Of course it varies with the state of the receiving set.... it is conditioned by the apparatus but not originated by it. If it were — if we knew that there was no human being at the microphone, we should not attend to the news. (*Mere Christianity*)

Furthermore, morality for Lewis is not an end in itself; in this sense he is not a moral absolutist:

> Though Christianity seems at first to be all about morality, all about duties and rules and guilt and virtue, yet it leads you on, out of all that, into something beyond. One has a glimpse of a country where they do not talk of those things, except perhaps as a joke. Every one there is filled full with what we should call goodness as a mirror is filled with light. But they do not call it goodness. They do not call it

anything. They are not thinking of it. They are too busy
looking at the source from which it comes. But this is near
the stage where the road passes over the rim of our world.
No one's eyes can see very far beyond that: lots of people's
eyes can see further than mine.

[Yet] God may be more than moral goodness: He is not
less. The road to the promised land runs past Sinai. The
moral law may exist to be transcended: but there is no
transcending it for those who have not first admitted its
claims upon them, and then tried with all their strength to
meet that claim, and fairly and squarely, faced the fact of
their failure. (*Ibid.*)

A final, and to my mind quite futile, charge against Lewis as
a conservative apologist for "mere Christianity" is that he is so
rational that he ignores human passions, so objective that he
ignores human subjectivity: in short, that he lacks the existential
dimension. This impression is received by readers of only his
systematic works; but his autobiography, more so his *Letters to
Malcolm* and his posthumously collected *Letters*, and most of all *A
Grief Observed*, reveal that Lewis can not only understand
experience through theology, but can also understand theology
through experience. How many Christians excel in both?

Before his marriage and the painful illness and eventual
death of his wife, reflected on in *A Grief Observed*, he could write
about the death of his closest friend:

No event has so corroborated my faith in the next world as
[Charles] Williams did simply by dying. When the idea of
death and the idea of Williams thus met in my mind, it was
the idea of death that was changed. (*Letters*)

But in *A Grief Observed* he notes that

It is hard to have patience with people who say 'There is no
death' or 'Death doesn't matter.' There is death. And
whatever is matters. And whatever happens has
consequences, and it and they are irrevocable and
irreversible. You might as well say that birth doesn't matter.

> I look up at the night sky. Is anything more certain than that in all those vast times and spaces, if I were allowed to search them, I should nowhere find her face, her voice, her touch? She died. She is dead. Is the word so difficult to learn? To say 'H. is dead' is to say 'All that is gone.' It is a part of the past. And the past is the past and that is what time means, and time itself is one more name for death.

He experiences not only death but also doubt:

> Sooner or later I must face the question in plain language. What reason have we, except our own desperate wishes, to believe that God is, by any standard we can conceive, 'good'? Doesn't all the prima facie evidence suggest exactly the opposite?

> Lord, are these your real terms? Can I meet H. again only if I learn to love you so much that I don't care whether I meet her or not? Consider, Lord, how it looks to us. What would anyone think of me if I said to the boys, 'No toffee now, But when you've grown up and don't really want toffee you shall have as much of it as you choose'?

But he questions himself, and not just God; and it is his objectivity that finally triumphs:

> The case is too plain. If my house has collapsed at one blow, that is because it was a house of cards. The faith which 'took these things into account' was not faith but imagination. . . . playing with innocuous counters labelled Illness, Pain, Death, and Loneliness. . . . You never know how much you really believe something until its truth or falsehood becomes a matter of life and death to you. . . . I thought I trusted the rope until it mattered tome whether it would bear me. Now it matters, and I find I didn't.

> But there are two questions here. In which sense may it [my faith] be a house of cards? Because the things I am believing are only a dream, or because I only dream that I believe them?

> Aren't all these notes the senseless writhings of a man who won't accept the fact that there is nothing we can do with suffering except to suffer it? . . . and now that I come to think of it, there's no practical problem before me at all. I know the two great commandments and I'd better get on with them. . . . What's left is not a problem about anything I could *do*. It's all about weights of feelings and motives and that sort of thing. It's a problem I'm setting myself. I don't believe God set it [to] me at all.

Lewis emerges neither with skepticism nor with comfort but with the "objectivity" with which he began, made existentially relevant through experience yet triumphantly transcending experience:

> My idea of God is not a divine idea. It has to be shattered time after time. He shatters it Himself. He is the great iconoclast. Could we not almost say that this shattering is one of the marks of His presence? The Incarnation is the supreme example. It leaves all previous ideas of the Messiah in ruins. And most are 'offended' by the iconoclasm; and blessed are those who are not. . . . All reality is iconoclastic. The earthly beloved, even in this life, incessantly triumphs over your mere idea of her. And you want her to; you want her with all her resistances, all her faults, all her unexpectedness. That is, in her foursquare and independent reality. . . . Not my idea of God, but God. Not my idea of H., but H. Yes, and also not my idea of my neighbour, but my neighbour.

This is no new Lewis: the experience of *A Grief Observed* does not contradict but corroborates the theology of *Miracles*:

> Men are reluctant to pass over from the notion of an abstract and negative deity to the living God. I do not wonder. Here lies the deepest tap-root of Pantheism and of the objection to traditional imagery. It was hated not, at bottom, because it pictured Him as man but because it pictured Him as king, or even as warrior. The Pantheist's God does nothing, demands nothing. He is there if you wish for Him, like a book on a shelf. He will not pursue you. There is no danger that at any time heaven and earth should flee away at his glance. If he were the truth, then we could

really say that all the Christian images of kingship were a historical accident of which our religion ought to be cleansed. It is with a shock that we discover them to be indispensable. You have had a shock like that before, in connection with smaller matters — when the line pulls at your hand, when something breathes beside you in the darkness. So here; the shock comes at the precise moment when the thrill of *life* is communicated to us along the clue we have been following. It is always shocking to meet life where we thought we were alone. 'Look out!' we cry, 'it's *alive*.' And therefore this is the very point at which so many draw back — I would have done so myself if I could — and proceed no further with Christianity. An 'impersonal God' — well and good. A subjective God of beauty, truth and goodness, inside our own heads — better still. A formless life-force surging through us, a vast power which we can tap — best of all. But God, Himself, alive, pulling at the other end of the cord, perhaps approaching at an infinite speed, the hunter, king, husband — that is quite another matter. There comes a moment when the children who have been playing at burglars hush suddenly: was that a *real* footstep in the hall? There comes a moment when people who have been dabbling in religion ('Man's search for God'!) suddenly draw back. Supposing we really found Him? We never meant it to come to *that*! Worse still, supposing He had found us?

Other Worlds: Lewis's Fiction

The fact that a Christian apologist's writing highly imaginative fiction surprises many people, surprises Lewis. "I do not think the resemblance between the Christian and the merely imaginative experience is accidental. I think that all things, in their way, reflect heavenly truth, the imagination not least." However, it may be thought that the resemblance between fantasy and Christianity lies in their both being forms of escapism; Lewis therefore offers a critical defense of the former as well as the latter:

(1) Fantasy is escapism only in the sense in which all fiction is escapism from present fact. To attack fantasy is to attack fiction; to defend fiction is to defend fantasy. Lewis's defense is

> that we seek an enlargement of our being. We want to be more than ourselves. Each of us by nature sees the whole world from one point of view. . . . to acquiesce in this particularity on the sensuous level — in other words, not to discount perspective — would be lunacy. . . . but we want to escape the illusions of perspective on higher levels too. . . . the man who is contented to be only himself, and therefore less a self, is in prison. (*An Experiment in Criticism*)

Far from dulling or emptying the actual world, fantasy deepens it: A man "does not despise real woods all real woods a little enchanted" ("On Three Ways of Writing for Children").

(2) Fantasy is in its own way realistic: "Nature has that in her which compels us to invent giants: and only giants will do." Talking beasts are "masks for Man, cartoons, parodies by Nature formed to reveal us." It is so-called realism, not fantasy, that fosters wishful thinking, escapism, and deception: "I never

47

expected the real world to be like the fairy tales. I think that I
did expect school to be like the school stories" (*ibid.*).

(3) Fantasy is a traditionally human form; for

> until quite modern times, nearly all stories were [non-
> realistic]. . . . Just as all except bores relate in conversation
> not what is normal but what is exceptional — you mention
> having seen a giraffe in Petty Cury, but don't mention
> having seen an undergraduate — so authors told of the
> exceptional. (*An Experiment in Criticism*)

Therefore "I side impenitently with the human race against the
modern reformer. Let there be wicked kings and beheadings,
battles and dungeons, giants and dragons, and let villains be
soundly killed at the end of the book" ("On Three Ways of
Writing for Children").

(4) Fantasy is not by nature fit only for children:

> The whole association of fairy tale and fantasy with
> childhood is local and accidental. I hope everyone has read
> Tolkien's essay on Fairy Tales, which is perhaps the most
> important contribution to the subject that anyone has yet
> made. If so, you will know already that, in most places and
> times, the fairy tale has not been specially made for, nor
> exclusively enjoyed by, children. It has gravitated to the
> nursery when it became unfashionable in literary circles, just
> as unfashionable furniture gravitated to the nursery in
> Victorian houses.

> Critics who treat *adult* as a term of approval, instead of as a
> merely descriptive term, cannot be adult themselves. To be
> concerned about being grown up, to admire the grown up
> because it is grown up, to blush at the suspicion of being
> childish; these things are the marks of childhood and
> adolescence.

> The modern view seems to me to involve a false conception
> of growth. They accuse us of arrested development because
> we have not lost a taste we had in childhood. But surely
> arrested development consists not in refusing to lose old
> things but in failing to add new things? . . . a tree grows

> because it adds rings; a train doesn't grow by leaving one
> station behind and puffing on to the next. . . . if to drop
> parcels and to leave stations behind were the essence and
> virtue of growth, why should we stop at the adult? Why
> should not *senile* be equally a term of approval? (*Ibid.*)

Lewis's fiction is not merely fantasy, however; he is one of the few writers who dares to concoct a myth. "*Out of the Silent Planet, Perelandra,* and *That Hideous Strength* were issued as 'novels,' but in reality they are three installments of one myth," observes Chad Walsh. What does this mean?

First of all, for Lewis "myth" is not an antonym to "truth." There is a kind of truth to a good myth that is different from, but no less true —more true, in fact — than fact: a fairy tale may be truer than a statistic. We can understand this kind of truth only from the experience of reading or hearing a great myth, like Lewis's or Tolkien's: when you close the covers of the book and look once again outside your apartment window, it seems overwhelmingly evident to you that you have not turned from fiction to reality but vice versa, from the more to the less real. A "willing suspension of disbelief" is required not for the world inside the myth but for the world outside it. How can we account for this power to move the intellectual will to believe unless the myth possesses some kind of truth? Tolkien explains it thus: "If he [the literary artist] indeed achieves a quality that can fairly be described by the dictionary definition: 'inner consistency of reality,' it is difficult to conceive how this can be, if the work does not in some way partake of reality" ("On Fairy Stories").

Lewis's explanation, in *Perelandra,* is itself mythical. Ransom finds that what is myth in one world is fact in another; that on pre-fallen Perelandra the distinction between myth and fact has not occurred; and that

> There is an environment of minds as well as of space. The
> universe is one — a spider's web wherein each mind lives
> along every line, a vast whispering gallery where (save for
> the direct action of Maleldil) though no news travels

unchanged yet no secret can be rigorously kept. In the mind of the fallen Archon under whom our planet groans, the memory of Deep Heaven and the Gods with whom he once consorted is still alive. Nay, in the very matter of our world, the traces of the celestial commonwealth are not quite lost. Memory passes through the womb and hovers in the air. The Muse is a real thing. A faint breath, as Virgil says, reaches even the late generations. Our mythology is based on a solider reality than we dream: but it is also at an almost infinite distance from that base.

But how is a good myth *more* real than "the real world"? Lewis's Platonic definition of symbolism in *The Allegory of Love* is the clue:

It is of the very nature of thought and language to represent what is immaterial in picturable terms. What is good or happy has always been high like the heavens and bright like the sun. Evil and misery were deep and dark from the first. . . . To ask how these married pairs of sensible and insensibles first came together would be of great folly; the real question is how they ever came apart. . . . This fundamental equivalence between the immaterial and the material may be used by the mind in two ways. . . . on the one hand you can start with an immaterial fact, such as the passions which you actually experience, and can then invent *visibilia* to express them. . . . this is allegory. . . . but there is another way of using the equivalence, which is almost the opposite of allegory, and which I would call sacramentalism or symbolism. If our passions, being immaterial, can be copied by material inventions, then it is possible that our material world in its turn is the copy of an invisible world. . . . The attempt to read that something else through its sensible imitations, to see the archetype in the copy, is what I mean by symbolism or sacramentalism. . . . The allegorist leaves the given — his own passions — to talk of that which is confessedly less real, which is a fiction. The symbolist leaves the given to find that which is more real. To put the difference in another way, for the symbolist it is we who are the allegory.

The same book explains the "higher realism" of Spenser in these terms:

> *The Faerie Queene* is 'like life' in a different sense. . . .. it is like life itself, not like the products of life. The things we read about in it are not like life, but the experience of reading it is like living. . . . his poetry has really tapped sources not easily accessible to discursive thought. He makes imaginable inner realities so vast and simple that they ordinarily escape us as the largely printed names of continents escape us on the map — too big for our notice, too visible for sight.

Lewis's own mythical achievements are three: his understanding of the nature of myth as such, in passages of literary criticism such as the preceding; his empathy with the medieval cosmological myth in *The Discarded Image*; and his creative use of the medieval myth as a foundation for his own mythic fiction. We must now consider this last area.

Lewis is best known for his overtly religious fiction. But *The Screwtape Letters*, *The Great Divorce*, and *The Pilgrim's Regress* are all allegorical rather than mythical, and really belong to apologetics more than to fiction. About his science fiction trilogy, however, he maintains that "a simple sense of wonder extraordinary things going on, were the motive forces behind the creation. . . . I've never started from a message or a moral. . . . the story itself should force its moral upon you" ("Unreal Estates"). Unlike most science fiction writers, Lewis writes not merely about other *worlds* but about *other* worlds: he is a master of this genre's peculiar virtue, the ability to expand our experience. One very small but typical example of this must suffice: the taste of fruit on Perelandra:

> It was so different from every other taste that it seemed mere pedantry to call it a taste at all. It was like the discovery of a totally new *genus* of pleasures, something unheard of among men, out of all reckoning, beyond all covenant. For one draught of this on earth wars would be

fought and nations betrayed. It could not be classified. He
could never tell us, when he came back to the world of men,
whether it was sharp or sweet, savoury or voluptuous,
creamy or piercing. 'Not like that' was all he could ever say
to such inquiries. . . . It appeared to him better not to taste
again. Perhaps the experience had been so complete that
repetition would be a vulgarity — like asking to hear the
same symphony twice in a day.

A more general "expansion of experience" is his conception of
"outer space" as full rather than empty:

> Now, with a certainty which never after deserted him, he
> saw the planets — the 'earths' he called them in his thought
> — as mere holes or gaps in the living heaven. . . . formed not
> by addition to but by subtraction from the surrounding
> brightness. . . . unless. . . . he groped for the idea. . . . unless
> visible light is also a hole or gap, a mere diminution of
> something else. Something that is to bright unchanging
> heaven as heaven is to the dark, heavy earths. . . . How
> indeed should it be otherwise, since out of this ocean the
> worlds and all their life had come? He had thought it
> barren: he saw now that it was the womb of the worlds. . . .
> space was the wrong name. Older thinkers had been wiser
> when they named it simply the heavens. (*Out of the Silent
> Planet*)

Though the works are novels and the protagonists men, the
most successful element in the trilogy are the eldils. Lewis has
done to angels what Tolkien has done to elves; as he himself
observes, "nothing less like the 'angel' of popular art could well
be imagined." One passage of simultaneous description and
explanation will suggest their nature; it illustrates also his
blending of medieval cosmology and modern physics in his new
cosmic myth. When Ransom asks a Malacandrian "sorn" whether
eldils have bodies, it replies:

> Body is movement. If it is at one speed, you smell
> something; if at another, you hear a sound; if at another, you
> see a sight; if at another, you neither see nor hear nor smell,

nor know the body in any way. But mark this, Small One, that the two ends meet. . . . if movement is faster, then that which moves is more nearly in two places at once. . . . but if the movement were faster still — it is difficult, for you do not know many words — you see that if you made it faster and faster, in the end the moving thing would be in all places at once. . . . Well, then, that is the thing at the top of all bodies — so fast that it is at rest, so truly body that it has ceased being body at all. But we will not talk of that. Start from where we are, Small One. The swiftest thing that touches our senses is light. We do not truly see light, we only see slower things lit by it, so that for us light is on the edge — the last thing we know before things become too swift for us. But the body of an *eldil* is a movement swift as light; you may say its body is made of light, but not of that which is light for the *eldil*. His 'light' is a swifter movement which for us is nothing at all; and what we call light is for him a thing like water, a visible thing, a thing he can touch and bathe in — even a dark thing when not illumined by the swifter. And what we call firm things — flesh and earth — seem to him thinner, and harder to see, than our light, and more like clouds, and nearly nothing. To us the *eldil* is a thin, half-real body that can go through walls and rocks: to himself he goes through them because he is solid and firm and they are like cloud. And what is true light to him and fills the heaven, so that he will plunge into the rays of the sun to refresh himself from it, is to us the black nothing in the sky at night. (*Ibid.*)

Till We Have Faces is not a myth in this cosmic sense, though it is labeled "a myth [Cupid and Psyche] retold." It is a "realistic" (historical) novel of conflicting myths: that of the Greek god of light, Apollonian reason, and that of Ungit the dark god of Dionysian blood and mystery. The god of light is not heavy enough, and Ungit is proved the wiser. Though we must avoid what Lewis calls "the personal heresy" (reading the writing through the writer rather than vice versa), we may note an obvious resemblance to Lewis's own rationalism-romanticism dilemma, his preference for the romantic, and his catalytic resolution through a higher revelation. The last is the point of

this book. Someone is said to have asked Bertrand Russell what
he would say to God if after death he found that God really
existed. Russell replied that he would ask Him why He hadn't
given us a little more evidence. To this excellent question Lewis
gives a surprisingly "developmental" answer. "I saw well why the
gods do not speak to us openly, nor let us answer. Till that word
can be dug out of us, why should they hear the babble that we
think we mean? How can they meet us face to face till we have
faces?"

The Chronicles of Narnia constitute another mythic cosmos,
simpler but even more successful, to my mind, than that of the
science fiction trilogy. These seven books are written for
children, and the protagonists are children; but by Lewis's own
critical dictum any children's story that cannot be read by adults
with pleasure and profit is not a good children's story either, but
a patronization, an attempt "to regale the child with things
calculated to please it but regarded by yourself with indifference
or contempt. The child, I am certain, would see through that."
Lewis respects children, as many modern children do not:

> 'Oh Susan!' said Jill, 'she's interested in nothing nowadays
> except nylons and lipstick and invitations. She always was a
> jolly sight too keen on being grown-up.' 'Grown-up indeed,'
> said the Lady Polly. 'I wish she *would* grow up. She wasted
> all her school time wanting to be the age she is now, and
> she'll waste all the rest of her life trying to stay that age.
> Her whole idea is to race on to the silliest time of one's life
> as quick as she can and then stop there as long as she can."
> (*The Last Battle*)

The Narnia books are called "dangerous" by Kathleen Nott
(no one more unsympathetic to Lewis than she has yet seen
print) because they contain not only little digs at modern foibles
such as the one above but also an overall theological allegory,
frustrating to the parent who likes the story but fears the child
may pick up some religious ideas subconsciously. (As Lewis
himself found out, "a young atheist cannot be too careful of his

reading.") Even Tolkien finds them "too allegorical." Yet their moral is not *imposed*. Lewis practises what he preaches, which is to let "the pictures tell you their own moral. For the moral inherent in them will rise from whatever spiritual roots you have succeeded in striking during the whole course of your life" ("On Three Ways of Writing for Children").

Perhaps this is why the Narnia books succeed with many readers to whom his formally apologetic essays and even his overtly religious allegories fail. Or perhaps, as Lewis says,

> the reason why the Passion of Aslan (lion-symbol of Christ) sometimes moves people more than the real story in the Gospels is. . . . that it takes them off their guard. In reading the real story, the fatal knowledge that one *ought* to feel in a certain way often inhibits the feeling. (*Letters*)

Or again, perhaps the simple change of names from "God" to "Aslan" or "Maleldil" lets us see behind the obscuring and encrusting veil not only of dull familiarity and religious associations but also that most convenient of all idols, the *word* "God."

Narnia's cosmos is true in the same mythic sense as that of the trilogy: it holds together as a world in itself, integral, consistent, and "astonishingly underivative." There is so much reality *in* it that the question of the reality outside it and of its relations to that latter reality need not even arise. A few chapter titles of the seven books, randomly arranged, will convey something of the atmosphere: "Deep Magic from the Dawn of Time"; "the Spell of the Utter East"; and "The Deplorable Word," which if spoken would destroy all of the speaker's world, leaving only himself. Lewis dares to describe without preciousness "a retired star," "drinkable light," and the wall at the world's end where the sky comes down to the earth. *The Last Battle*, last and greatest of the seven, simply bursts its bounds; never, I believe, has there been a children's story like it. Like its Arthurian predecessor (its title is from Malory's famous last chapter), its

theme is the archetypal End of the World, End of the Old Order.
The Giant Time wakes, the sky falls, and Aslan calls home the
stars in a reversal of the progression of Creation (which Lewis
has also dared to describe in *The Magician's Nephew*). The plot
leading to such a denouement parallels that of *That Hideous
Strength*: men usurping the place of God "have pulled down
Deep Heaven upon their heads." The problem, however, is that
of *Till We Have Faces*: the divine silence; and the fear is that of *A
Grief Observed*: the Cosmic Sadist, "this horrible fear that Aslan
has come and is not like the Aslan we have believed in and hoped
for. . . . it is as if the sun rose one day and were a black sun. . . .
this is the end of all things." But its concluding Heaven is as deep
as the pit from which it is the rescue: total despair leads to total
Joy. More than any other, this book is the apotheosis of Lewis's
works. Its themes are his major themes; its medium is his most
successful medium; and its personality is his personality.

Despite Lewis's own critical dictum that evaluative criticism,
and especially adverse criticism, is one of the most difficult and
least rewarding literary tasks, I should like to venture some
general judgments on his fiction. By conventional standards, the
greatest weakness of Lewis's fiction is certainly his
characterization. He is at his best in the least intimate and
personal scenes; he describes his villains better than his heroes,
damnation better than salvation, strange men better than
ordinary men, inhabitants of other planets better than those of
earth, and even *eldils* better than human beings. He seems like
the feudal French peasant who knew more of the geography of
Hell than of France. A further problem is his rationalism. A
style as suitable to apologetic essays as Lewis's can hardly be
suitable to fiction. Because Lewis's writing is so very rational,
one gets the impression that his characters are all very rational.
Worse, he often gives reasons instead of motives, rarely
attempting to even acknowledge the existence of subconscious
motivation, and often seems to *use* his characters as bearers of
philosophical points, often by means of rational, expository

conversations, rather than as objects of the author's interest for their own sake.

Such a basic charge can be met only by an equally basic defense, and Lewis has one: he is writing a different *kind* of novel than is usually written today:

> It may very well be convenient not to call such things novels. If you prefer, call them a very special form of novels. Either way, the conclusion will be much the same: they are to be tried by their own rules. It is absurd to condemn them because they do not often display any deep or sensitive characterization. They oughtn't to. It is a fault if they do.... Every good writer knows that the more unusual the scenes and events of his story are, the slighter, the more ordinary, the more typical his persons should be. Hence Gulliver is a commonplace little man and Alice a commonplace little girl. If they had been more remarkable they would have wrecked their books. The Ancient Mariner himself is a very ordinary man. To tell how odd things struck odd people is to have an oddity too much: he who is to see strange sights must not himself be strange. ("On Science Fiction")

Lewis does not write "realism" but epic — "higher realism." Stella Gibbons says:

> I wish that Lewis could have written a 'straight' novel in a modern setting, but perhaps his mind, soaked since boyhood in saga and myth, could find no patience with modern people and their small dramas. He seems to have been perpetually haunted by the realities lying behind appearances. ("Imaginative Writing" in *Of Other Worlds*)

In this type of Spenserian, Platonic, archetypal, mythic fiction,

> the plot, as we call it, is only really a net whereby to catch something else. The real theme may be, and perhaps usually is, something that has no sequence in it, something other than a process and much more like a state or quality. Giantship, otherness, the desolation of space, are examples that have crossed our path. The titles of some stories

illustrate the point very well. *The Well at the World's End* — can a man write a story to that title? ("On Stories")

Thus *Perelandra* is not about Ransom, or his adventures, or the Fall, but about Perelandra; and *That Hideous Strength* is about that hideous strength! Lewis burns his archetypes into our brains like Ingmar Bergman's visual images: what reader can forget *Perelandra's* Eden of floating islands, or in *That Hideous Strength* the anti-utopia of a planet-wide machine sterile of all organic life, a lunar "freedom from Nature"? Lewis dares to describe even gods in passages of great suggestive power, such as the following:

> 'It must be cold outside,' said Dimble. All thought of that: of stiff grass, hen-roosts, dark places in the middle of woods, graves. Then of the sun's dying, the Earth gripped, suffocated, in airless cold, the black sky lit only with stars. And then, not even stars: the heat-death of the universe, utter and final blackness of nonentity from which Nature knows no return. Another life? ... But the old life gone, all its times, all its hours and days, gone. Can even Omnipotence *bring back*? Where do years go, and why? Man would never understand it. The misgiving deepened. Perhaps there was nothing to be understood.
>
> Saturn, whose name in the heavens is Lurga, stood in the Blue Room. His spirit lay upon the house, or even on the whole earth, with a cold pressure such as might flatten the very orb of Tellus to a wafer. (*That Hideous Strength*)

But a novel cannot be all epic; and though in the large Lewis's combination of romanticism with rationalism, imagination with philosophy, is a rich one, yet in the small, in such details as the didactic conversations, the reader often feels lectured to. Lewis never fully resolved his basic dualism of rationalism and romanticism: his philosophy is better put in his philosophical works and his fiction is best when the philosophy is so implicit in the simple beauty of the story or setting that extraction is impossible.

Finally, in minimizing Lewis's characterizations we must not forget his supreme success: few writers of fiction *or* apologetics, and far fewer writers of both, have portrayed as compellingly attractive a God as Lewis has dared to portray. No God farther from the God of undersexed seminarians could be imagined: regal, male, and glorious. Like Aslan, "of course he isn't *safe*. But he's good."

The Last Dinosaur:
Lewis's Historical Significance

Even by the standards of fiction, Lewis's religious writings are his greatest because their character and their story are the greatest. His religious achievement finds a surprising parallel, I believe, in Kierkegaard: surprising because Lewis is far too objective and rationalistic to be labeled an "existentialist," but parallel for a number of reasons.

First among them is the fact that Lewis, like Kierkegaard, lived and wrote according to the maxim "purity of heart is to will one thing"; and that "one thing" was "mere Christianity" for Lewis as it was for Kierkegaard. Like Kierkegaard, Lewis disdained the Hegelian attempt to "go beyond" Christianity and to relativize it. The paradoxical result is that the apparently narrower, "mere" Christianity turns out to be so large as to be cosmic. Lewis need not venture out of it into more inclusive realms because he finds it inclusive of other realms. As Chesterton says in his parable "The World Inside Out," the Church is not in the world; the world is in the Church.

Austin Farrer summarizes Lewis's achievement nicely:

> he provided a positive exhibition of the force of Christian ideas morally, imaginatively, and rationally [the good, the beautiful, and the true: what other standards are there?]. The strength of his appeal. . . . lies in the many-sidedness of his work. ("The Christian Apologist" in *Light on C.S. Lewis*)

Who can excel Lewis in all three departments? What Christian makes Christianity more morally compelling, more imaginatively moving, *and* more rationally convincing? Having many strings to his bow improves the tone of each one: professional preaching, for example, is nearly always bad preaching. And because of

Lewis's unprofessional, many-sided excellence, he is one of the few religious writers who is read by lowbrows and highbrows, poets and philosophers, conservatives and liberals, Catholics and Protestants, Christians and non-Christians. Though many communicate to a larger audience, few communicate to a more diversified one.

Modern man's crisis, all seem agreed, is one of disintegration, of alienation. He has split his own being, having split it from its source and center; and he finds his reason detached from his heart, the sciences from the humanities, analytic philosophy from existential philosophy (the navigators have crossed the Channel and forgotten to take their ship), producing more and more men who are either computers or psychedelomaniacs. Lewis's romantic rationalism shows that the two mental hemispheres *can* coexist happily and fruitfully in one man and one philosophy.

I am sure Lewis himself would insist that his most important single achievement is his *least* original: his re-presentation of "mere Christianity" to an age so eager to build contemporary Christianities that it seems bored with the foundation of the buildings. In an age of religious mixed drinks, Lewis takes his straight; he opposes "Christianity-and-water." In an age of religious pioneers and frontier Christians, Lewis is the most intelligent and imaginative tender of the home front, and the best refutation of the gibe that a twentieth-century Christian can be honest, or intelligent, or orthodox, or any two of the three, but not all three.

Lewis is certainly no twentieth-century Aquinas. Neither a professional philosopher nor a professional theologian, he offers no new philosophy or theology. But he more than attains the modest goal he sets for himself. He "does his thing" — the sort of thing usually done only by second and third rate writers (and, more importantly, second and third rate thinkers). It is an important thing; for he speaks to the intelligent masses, not to the bored scholar who is searching for originality. His popularity among the scholarly establishment is minimal in an age which demands originality above all. He cannot compare in radical originality with movements like death-of-God Christianity or Marxist Christianity. One wonders, however, whether such movements would ever have seen the light of day if their authors had "seen the light" — that is, been familiar with Lewis's "mere Christianity" instead of either the "Christianity-and-water" or the "Christianity-and-fire" against which they react.

Like Kierkegaard, Lewis appears to many to be an innovator by differing from his age. And like Kierkegaard's, Lewis's difference with his age is usually misunderstood by well-intentioned spirits of the age who wish to pay him the only compliment they know. He is half-serious when he says: "What I do is to recall, as well as I can, what my mother used to say on the subject, eke it out with a few similar thoughts of my own, and so produce what would have been strict orthodoxy in about 1900. and this seems to them outrageously *avant garde* stuff."

Yet Lewis's real originality cannot be hidden, even when he disclaims it; and it is a significant paradox that a man who so consistently disclaims originality should so consistently be praised for it. This fact, taken together with the correlative fact that those Christian writers who strive most desperately to be original succeed least, write exceedingly dull books, and produce warmed-over Comte, Hegel, Marx, Freud, or Teilhard, reveals something not merely about Lewis but also about originality. To quote Lewis's own dictum again:

> No man who bothers about originality will ever be original: whereas if you simply try to tell the truth (without caring twopence how often it has been told before) you will, nine times out of ten, become original without ever having noticed it. The principle runs through all life from top to bottom. Give up your self and you will find your real self. (*Mere Christianity*)

I have found that most readers who dislike Lewis dislike him violently. They find him irksome, unsettling, even unendurable.

When the reason for this dislike is analyzed, it usually turns out
to be one of the following: (1) "he's too rationalistic" (that is, he
makes the uncomfortable demand that what we dare call our
thoughts be "baized" on something); (2) "he's too romantic, too
sentimental" (that is, since his *expression* of sentiment is not
sentimental, the critic must prefer either sentimental expression
of unsentimental consciousness or no sentiment at all); (3) "he's
too fantastic" (that is, too imaginative for me, who already know
the boundaries of reality); (4) "he's too moralistic" (that is, I can't
take his strong meat when so many attractive excuses abound); or
(5) "he's too religious." This last becomes what can only be called
an ultimate disagreement once it is realized that Lewis is *not*
"religious," but godly. Once again Kierkegaard offers a parallel
with his notion of "the offence": those who have followed the
Great Offender most closely have always been closest to His holy
unpopularity. The violent opposition Lewis generates in critics
like Kathleen Nott is exactly what we would expect if a "mere
Christian" came to post-Christian England.

A more valid criticism, I believe, is that Lewis is the victim
of his many-sidedness. The many-sided man runs the risk of
disunity; and while no one could say that Lewis has no principle
of unity or that this Christian center is not related to his many
sides (many think it too closely related, and his work too
didactic), one could say that the sides are not related to each
other, that Lewis never fully resolved his youthful dilemma
between rationalism and romanticism. Each of these two forces
in him is so strong that it would take a giant to fuse them: Lewis
is an elf, but not a giant. Though his rational apologetics do not
lack imagination and his imaginative novels do not lack
rationality, yet the two elements are not fully fused in either
medium. Even his great imagination does not fully overcome the
abstract apriorism of his apologetics, and even his rationality
does not fully overcome the remoteness from ordinary life of his
novels. Though *he* does not lack human sympathy, his reason
does, so that Austin Farrer must say about *The Problem of Pain*:

"when under suffering we see good men go to pieces we do not witness the failure of a moral discipline to take effect; we witness the advance of death." And it is significant that his imagination needs fictional outlet: does this perhaps indicate that he never quite solved his pre-Christian dilemma ("nearly all that I loved I believed to be imaginary; nearly all that I believed to be real I thought grim and meaningless")?

This criticism immediately suggests another: does not the fact that his imagination is fictional mean that his imaginative world-view is unlivable in the real world? Eldils *are* irrelevant to subway strikes and fair housing laws, however much more interesting. It is difficult to imagine a Harlem slum dweller "relating" to Lewis (though whether this is too bad for Lewis or too bad for Harlem is another question). Lewis tells us how to live in his fictional worlds, in the medieval world, even in any world ("mere Christian" ethics), but not how to live in *this* world. He offers no Christian sociology, politics, or economics.

Three answers may be given to this criticism. First and most simply, no one man can be expected to do everything! Second, the critic implicitly prefers relevance to truth. Thirdly, it is even Lewis's irrelevance that makes him relevant; for when "relevance" becomes a god, the relevant thing to do is to smash the idol. In an age of uncertainty, one more ringing declaration of uncertainties is surely less relevant than the certainty which the seekers claim to be seeking — unless seeking is not for the sake of finding. An open mind, like an open door, is indispensable, but as a means, not an end. How if after the awaited guest entered, the door were left open for him to depart? Openness to truth is one thing; openness to openness quite another. The latter is like faith in faith instead of faith in God, or being in love with love instead of with an individual.

Lewis's historical significance, then, is belied by the unpopularity of his cause. To embrace "mere Christianity" is not to abandon the twentieth century any more than to embrace an equally unpopular and an equally mere Christianity in the second or third centuries was to abandon that similarly critical and similarly dying age. One of the reasons the modern world lacks enthusiasm for Christianity is surely that Christians lack enthusiasm for Christianity ("the best argument against Christianity is Christians"). When a collective inferiority complex moves Christians to compete in saying to the non-Christian "Look, I'm the same as you; my philosophy of life doesn't really differ from yours: isn't it wonderful?" the non-Christian quite naturally replies "No; frankly, you bore me." No one buys a product because it's like every other product, but because it's different.

But I have insisted that it is misleading to label Lewis a "conservative." That designation, striving to be anti-modern, actually succumbs to modernity both because it is a modern, not a pre-modern, term, and because it defines itself over against modernity rather than in its own terms (just as nothing admits the greatness of Communism so much as a whole philosophy of anticommunism). Lewis's escape from this age and its labels makes him most relevant to the age; for when nearly everything ideational is polarized into "conservative" and "liberal," someone like Lewis is living proof of the limitations of these categories. Though the content of his position is not that of liberalism, its imagination, its eschatology, its mysticism, its cosmic sweep, and its confidence in reason make it impossible to classify him with any of the conservative stereotypes, at least in this country: the gruff, realistic New England farmer, the sweet, fearful Midwestern matron, the cynical, selfish Eastern businessman, the fanatical, sectarian Southwestern preacher, or the bullheaded, rednecked Southern bigot (caricatures all, it may be; but the point is that Lewis is not even thus caricaturable).

Both "conservative" and "liberal" are a priori structures, humanly — even politically — manufactured artifices; both "conservative Christianity" and "liberal Christianity" are "Christianity-ands," human interpretation. Lewis's "mere Christianity" is, by contrast, a divine irruption: if a label is needed, "confrontation Christianity" might do. And here is another parallel between Lewis and Kierkegaard: the Divine Surprise. The God who is no function of human reason, or human aspirations, or human *anything*, creeps up behind us. He is the God of miracles, and He is Himself a miracle, something that "slaps us in the face." We must respond, either by accepting Him, rejecting Him, or avoiding Him.

Lewis's significance for the twentieth century, even his critics must admit, is at least that of a test case, a rock on which new philosophies may break, a Christianity against which the new Christianities must be fairly and unprejudicedly compared. If the new ships can get past the old rock, they will have smooth sailing. But hundreds of such ships have foundered in previous ages on such a rock. "Mere Christianity" has died many times, and always buried its undertakers; it has often gone to the dogs, and it was always the dogs that died (if Chesterton will permit me to borrow once more).

At the very least, then, Lewis is significant as a "last dinosaur," as he put it himself in his inaugural lecture at Cambridge:

> I myself belong far more to that Old Western order than to yours. . . . I would give a good deal to hear any ancient Athenian, even a stupid one, talking about Greek tragedy. He would know in his bones so much that we seek in vain. . . . Ladies and gentlemen, I stand before you somewhat as that Athenian might stand. I read as a native texts that you must read as foreigners. You see why I said that the claim was not really arrogant; who can be proud of speaking fluently his mother's tongue or knowing his way about his father's house? It is my settled conviction that in order to read Old Western literature you must suspend most of the responses and unlearn most of the habits you have acquired in reading modern literature. And because this is the judgment of a native, I claim that, even if the defense of my convictions is weak, the fact of my conviction is a historical datum, to which you should give full weight. That way, where I fail as a critic, I may yet be useful as a specimen. I

> would even dare to go further. Speaking not only for myself
> but for all other Old Western men whom you may meet, I
> would say, use your specimens while you can. There are not
> going to be many more dinosaurs. ("De Descriptione
> Temporum")

Lewis's conscious defense of a tradition could appear only at the
end of that tradition, at its dissolution, when it is set off from its
new opposite (just as Church theology gets defined only over
against heresies). If Christianity is not dying, Old Western Man
is, and John LawlOr may be right to say of Lewis: "It is as certain
as these things can be that we shall not see another like him"
("The Tutor and the Scholar" in *Light on C.S. Lewis*). If so, great
things are dying forever, and we can only hope that greater, not
smaller things will replace them.

Select Bibliography

In compiling this bibliography I have used the unscholarly but practical device of anticipating the reader's likely interests. To this end, I have (1) listed American rather than British editions, (2) listed paperback rather than hardcover editions wherever available, (3) arranged the books by genre, and (4) ordered them within each genre not alphabetically but according to my judgment of descending rank of interest and quality.

PERSONAL
Surprised By Joy: The Shape of My Early Life. New York: Harcourt, Brace, Jovanovich, 1966.
A Grief Observed. New York: Bantam, 1976.
Letters, W.H. Lewis, ed. New York: Harcourt, Brace, Jovanovich, 1966.
Letters to an American Lady. Grand Rapids: Eerdmans, 1967.

LITERARY HISTORY AND CRITICISM
The Discarded Image: An Introduction to Medieval and Renaissance Literature. Cambridge: Cambridge University Press, 1964.
A Preface to 'Paradise Lost'. New York: Oxford University Press, 1942.
The Allegory of Love: A Study in Medieval Tradition. New York: Oxford University Press, 1936.
An Experiment in Criticism. New York: Cambridge University Press, 1961.
Studies in Words. Cambridge: Cambridge University Press, 1960.
English Literature in the Sixteenth Century, Excluding Drama (Volume III of *The Oxford History of English Literature*). Oxford: Clarendon Press, 1954.
On Stories and Other Essays on Literature. New York: Harcourt, Brace, Jovanovich, 1982.

RELIGIOUS STUDIES
Mere Christianity. New York: Macmillan, 1978.
The Problem of Pain. New York: Macmillan, 1978.
Miracles: A Preliminary Study. New York: Macmillan, 1978.
The Screwtape Letters. New York: Macmillan, 1982.

The Four Loves. New York: Harcourt, Brace, Jovanovich, 1971.
Letters to Malcolm: Chiefly on Prayer. New York: Harcourt, Brace, Jovanovich, 1973.
Reflections on the Psalms. New York: Walker & Co., 1985.

PHILOSOPHY
The Abolition of Man. New York: Macmillan, 1978.

COLLECTIONS OF ESSAYS
The Weight of Glory and Other Addresses. New York: Macmillan, 1980.
God in the Dock. Grand Rapids: Eerdmans, 1970.
Christian Reflections. Grand Rapids: Eerdmans, 1968.
The World's Last Night and Other Essays. New York: Harcourt, Brace, Jovanovich, 1973.
Present Concerns. New York: Harcourt, Brace, Jovanovich, 1975.
Of Other Worlds: Essays and Stories. New York: Harcourt, Brace, Jovanovich, 1975.

POEMS
Poems. New York: Harcourt, Brace, Jovanovich, 1977.
Narrative Poems. New York: Harcourt, Brace, Jovanovich, 1979.

FICTION
Till We Have Faces: A Myth Retold. New York: Harcourt, Brace, Jovanovich, 1980.
The Great Divorce. New York: Macmillan, 1978.
The Space Trilogy, 3 vols., including *Out of the Silent Planet, Perelandra,* and *That Hideous Strength.* New York: Macmillan, 1986.
The Pilgrim's Regress: An Allegorical Apology for Christianity, Reason, and Romanticism. New York: Bantam, 1981.

CHILDREN'S FICTION
The Chronicles of Narnia, 7 books, including *The Lion, the Witch and the Wardrobe, Prince Caspian, The Voyage of the 'Dawn Treader', The Silver Chair, The Horse and His Boy, The Magician's Nephew,* and *The Last Battle.* New York: Macmillan, 1986.

SELECTED SECONDARY SOURCES
Christopher, Joe R. *C.S. Lewis: An Annotated Checklist.* Kent, OH: Kent State University Press, 1964.
Green, Roger Lancelyn. *C.S. Lewis, A Biography.* New York: Harcourt, Brace, Jovanovich, 1974.

Schakel, Peter J. *Reason and Imagination in C.S. Lewis.* Grand Rapids: Eerdmans, 1984.

Howard, Thomas. *The Achievement of C.S. Lewis.* Wheaton, IL: Harold Shaw, 1980.

Ford, Paul. *Companion to Narnia.* San Francisco: Harper & Row, 1980.

Purtill, Richard J. *C.S. Lewis' Case for the Christian Faith.* Grand Rapids: Eerdmans, 1980.

Kilby, Clyde. *The Christian World of C.S. Lewis.* Grand Rapids: Eerdmans, 1964.

Schakel, Peter J., ed. *The Longing for a Form: Essays on the Fiction of C.S. Lewis.* Kent, OH: Kent State University Press, 1977.